The Sea Power Library

CRUISERS

The Sea Power Library

CRUISERS

by Jonathan Rawlinson

Rourke Publications, Inc.
Vero Beach, Florida 32964

The powerful cruiser of today's modern navy has a vital role to play in the passage of free trade on the world's oceans.

Library of Congress Cataloging-in-Publication Data
Rawlinson, Jonathan, 1944-
   Cruisers/by Jonathan Rawlinson.
   p. cm. — (The Sea power library)
   Includes index.
   ISBN 0-86625-085-9
   1. Cruisers (Warships) — United States — Juvenile literature.
2. Cruisers (Warships) — Soviet Union — Juvenile literature.
3. Cruisers (Warships) Juvenile literature. I. Title.
II. Series.
V820.3R39   1989   88-31466
359.3'253 - dc19   CIP
                            AC

Contents

The Role Of The Cruiser

Built at the end of World War Two, the USS Albany was converted from gun to missile armament in the early 1960s.

For more than a hundred years after the Declaration of Independence, the United States remained isolated from other countries. North America has vast natural resources, and the needs of the pioneers and early nation builders were not great. Moreover, the countries of central Europe, where most immigrants came from, were continually at war, and the U.S. did not want to fight battles in far-off countries. There were enough challenges on the new frontier without rushing to the aid of old political systems that many pioneers had come to America to escape.

During the late nineteenth century, tension in Europe reached a high point. Science and technology were playing an important role in developing greater war machines than the world had ever seen before. Britain and Germany had great empires, and the way to protect their interests was through the use of sea power on a gigantic scale. With the introduction of steam toward the end of the century, warships became much more powerful instruments of foreign policy.

Early in the twentieth century, Britain introduced the Dreadnought class of heavy, ironclad battleships. With a speed of 21 **knots** and ten 12-inch guns capable of hitting targets almost four miles away, these giants displaced 18,000 tons and were the most feared ships of their day. They led in turn to the giant warships of World War Two that threatened supply routes and the movement of merchant shipping. Supplies were vital, and the needs of America's allies in that war for food and munitions proved how important it was to keep the sea lanes open.

Built between 1962 and 1967, the five ships of the Belknap class were steam-powered and those remaining in service are imposing and well armed ships.

Today the United States is no longer isolated. The vast industrial machinery of her production lines and factories must be fed by natural resources that cannot be found exclusively on American soil. For many decades the United States produced more raw materials than its growing industrial complex could use. Now the U.S. is deficient in raw materials and must rely heavily on foreign imports.

Outside China and the Soviet Union, almost half the world's mineral production is delivered to U.S. factories for the manufacture of goods and products. Many U.S. products manufactured in American factories are exported to countries that need complex machinery or pieces of equipment they cannot get elsewhere. The vast quantity of imports to the U.S. and the movement of goods across the world rely mainly on shipping for their transportation.

California-class boats displace more than 11,000 tons fully loaded and carry a pad for two helicopters, housed at the rear of the ship.

The Leahy class introduced the "Mack", the combined mast and smoke stack, with pipes emerging on the rear side of two plated masts.

The USS South Carolina was the second of six California-class ships built between 1970 and 1980, each with two water-cooled nuclear reactors.

The cruiser USS Vincennnes *packs a powerful punch using the Aegis weapons control system for air defense.*

Three powerful Ticonderoga-class cruisers lie berthed ready for duty. ▼

Each year the U.S. imports goods worth $250,000 million, and more than 18 million people are employed in the import-export business. Almost all the **bauxite** we use to manufacture aluminum for pots, pans, and engines comes from abroad. All the rubber we use for tires, wire insulation, and medical tools comes from Southeast Asia. More than 75 percent of the nickel used to make aircraft parts, turbines, nuclear reactors, and electronic devices is imported.

In all, the U.S. has 93 basic materials on what is called a "strategic" list. These materials are absolutely vital for U.S. trade and industry. The U.S. imports 84 percent of the top 19 items on the strategic materials list. It is important that these items are shipped to the U.S. regularly. Just as ironclad battleships of old helped preserve vast empires, so do U.S. warships ensure the passage of free trade to and from many countries around the world.

The U.S. merchant fleet has almost 2,000 ships bringing vital materials to American ports and sending manufactured goods overseas. Ships are needed to protect these vessels from blackmail or surprise attack. If left totally unprotected, these ships could be caught in small wars or local conflicts and come under attack, as many ships have in the Persian Gulf, for instance. It is because the U.S. Navy has a continuing role in peacetime as well as war that ships are built for a variety of functions. Not all of them are to do with all-out war.

Throughout naval history, the free-ranging warship has had the greatest success of all. Many warships are designed to operate as part of a battle group involving many other ships. Some, like gunboats, patrol inland waters or estuaries to protect isolated coastal communities or to police difficult stretches of sparsely populated shoreline. Yet the vessel that embodies all the classic features of a warship is the most difficult of all to define. Capable of operating on its own, it is large, powerful, fast, and heavily defended. It is the cruiser, a ship that has changed its role many times in the last century.

The cruiser owes its origin to frigates of the eighteenth and nineteenth centuries, where first sail and then steam provided power for independent operations protecting friendly ships or "cruising" to the attack. Toward the end of the nineteenth century, these two duties were separated into two main types

of cruisers. Heavy, long-range ships protected the ocean-going merchant fleet while smaller ships were built to hunt battle fleets.

There is potentially a big gap between giant battleships and cruisers. Battleships have a typical **displacement** of more than 40,000 tons, and cruisers, of between 10,000 tons and 15,000 tons. During the 1920s, the U.S. and Japan each needed cruisers to police their merchant fleets in the Pacific Ocean. A treaty limiting cruisers to 10,000 tons was made, although most European countries opted for 8,000-ton cruisers, which were lighter and faster. The Germans, however, continued to build bigger ships. Under the political control of Adolf Hitler, their navy soon had heavy cruisers like the *Prinz Eugen,* with a maximum displacement of more than 18,000 tons.

Treaties were torn up when the Germans attacked neighboring countries in 1939 and the Japanese attacked the U.S. at Pearl Harbor in 1941. So big were the German heavy cruisers that they were popularly called "pocket battleships." For a while the U.S. was

The United States presently operates 45 cruisers in every major ocean of the world, helping to protect merchant ships and prevent aggression.

tempted to build heavy cruisers. In December 1941, the month Japan attacked the Pearl Harbor naval base, construction began on a giant cruiser.

Based on false intelligence that Japan was developing fast surface raiders, the Alaska class was laid down with a length of 808 feet and a loaded displacement of more than 34,000 tons! Two ships were built, and they served in the Pacific for a few months before the unconditional surrender of Japan in September 1945. Both were scrapped in 1961.

The **Ticonderoga-class** *warship is one of the most heavily armed fighting ships in the world and is frequently called upon to provide protection to battle groups.*

USS Yorktown, *a Ticonderoga-class cruiser, shows her flat stern.*

Leahy And Bainbridge Classes

Of the 40 cruisers in active service with the U.S. Navy at the end of 1988, 10 are in the Leahy and Bainbridge classes. They represent the first of the modern-cruiser family brought about by the development of missiles and anti-ship weapons. Today, the navy operates nine Leahy class and one Bainbridge ship. They were laid down in a program of construction that began in 1959 and were commissioned between 1962 and 1964.

Shortly after World War Two ended in 1945, the cruiser was believed by some to have reached the

The Leahy-class USS England shows off her starboard bow and two Terrier surface-to-air missiles.

end of its useful life. Battleships were thought to be too large and cumbersome for the fast patrol and attack duties which had been developed to near perfection by the time hostilities ended. Cruisers did, however, get a new lease of confidence when they were used to hit land targets during the Korean War (1950-53).

Although built almost thirty years ago, the USS Worden *[Leahy class] was rated as a guided-missile cruiser in June 1975.*

By the mid-1950s, outstanding developments in rockets and guided missiles served once more to make large ships vulnerable, all except the cruisers. They were the only ships large enough to carry heavy equipment yet not too big to show a high turn of speed and good maneuverability. At first missiles were used for fleet defense as protection against air attack; World War Two had shown how vulnerable ships were to planes and carrier groups. Then missiles were designed to attack surface targets, and in 1960 the Soviet navy laid down the Kynda-class cruiser equipped with surface-to-surface missiles (**SSM**).

The Leahy was the first U.S. class specifically designed for missile warfare. It ushered in the new age of warships without guns and gave the cruiser a completely new lease on life. The Leahy ships did have two 76mm (3-inch) guns, but they were there

Bainbridge *carries out a high-speed turn on exercise.*

The USS Reeves *at speed on a quiet sea.*

simply because no one could seriously think of building a warship without them! Primary armament consisted of twin launchers, one fore and one aft, for the Terrier surface-to-air missile (**SAM**). Very little anti-submarine warfare (**ASW**) equipment was carried because the ship was designed as a screen for fast carrier attack forces. It was, however, fitted with twin torpedo tubes.

Leahy ships are 533 feet long and have a maximum loaded displacement of 8,200 tons and a top speed of almost 33 knots. Modifications have subsequently changed the armament. These ships now have 80 Standard missiles for the two twin launchers and eight Harpoon surface-to-surface missiles for ship attack. In this guise they were redesignated in 1975 as guided-missile cruisers. ASW rockets are also fitted, capable of firing torpedoes or nuclear depth charges. The 76mm guns have gone, replaced by Phalanx for close-range defense against anti-ship missiles.

The *Bainbridge* is essentially similar in design to the Leahy-class ships although it is slightly larger to accommodate a nuclear propulsion unit. It was the third nuclear-powered ship for the U.S. Navy, preceded by the cruiser *Long Beach* and the carrier *Enterprise.* Leahy- and Bainbridge-class ships have a crew complement of 423 and 558, repectively. At 30 knots, *Bainbridge* is marginally slower than the Leahy class. The navy usually operates six Leahy-class cruisers in the Pacific and three Leahy and the *Bainbridge* in the Atlantic.

The smooth lines of the Leahy class display a distinct family resemblance to the Bainbridge and Truxtun, of which they are small versions.

USS *Long Beach*

With a maximum loaded displacement of 17,500 tons, the **USS** *Long Beach* was the first U.S. cruiser built after World War Two. It was the first ship with an all-missile armament and, perhaps most important of all, the first nuclear-powered surface warship in the world. The combination of these two powerful technologies characterizes the best in modern naval applications: the ship as a launch platform for sophisticated and extremely fast weapons, and a propulsion system that gives the ship endurance, range, and a long time on duty.

One unfortunate consequence of modern technology and its fast pace of progress is that it soon renders its own inventions obsolete. The *Long Beach* was expensive to build and must be kept in service for several decades, while the technology that brought it about moves on and improves. *Long Beach* began as the design for a 7,800-ton frigate. Then it was

Built between 1957 and 1961, the USS Long Beach *was the world's first nuclear-powered cruiser, although only* ▶ *one of this type was built and the ship is now considered rather dated.*

The USS Turner *shows her aft deck, used for operating LAMPS helicopters.*

19

assigned the Regulus II cruise missile, which was a sea-launched weapon of the 1950s, 57 feet long and powered by a General Electric turbojet engine. The missile was canceled, and the Long Beach design was adapted to incorporate the Talos SAM system. Space was even reserved for eight Polaris ballistic missiles, the same type designed for the vertical launch tubes of submerged submarines! That idea was soon scrapped. The most radical, and sensible, idea attached to the *Long Beach* was the nuclear reactor. The engines use turbines powered by nuclear reactors that do not need fuel to burn. Conventional, oil-burning engines are limited in range by the amount of oil they can carry or by the number of times they can be refueled at sea.

By 1956 the design had grown to a displacement of 11,000 tons. When finally launched in 1959, *Long Beach* had a standard operating displacement of 15,540 tons. As the first of her kind, she was an important ship in the fleet. Her reactor, though, was soon outdated by more refined designs, and she remains the only one of her class. *Long Beach* is 721 feet in length, with a beam of 73 feet. She carries a complement of 65 officers and 893 enlisted men during her patrols, which are usually in the Pacific Ocean.

Long Beach has eight Harpoon and eight Tomahawk missiles for attacking surface or land targets, Terrier and Standard SAM rounds, twin 127mm (5-inch) guns, two Phalanx point defense weapons, and one ASW rocket launcher. Although a helicopter pad is attached to the aft deck, *Long Beach* has only modest provision for a helicopter. As recently as 1985, the ship received additional side armor when the boxed Tomahawk launchers were fitted. Each of the two reactors are similar in design to the eight fitted to the carrier USS *Enterprise*.

Long Beach spends most of her duty time in the Pacific Ocean and will serve the U.S. Navy for another 15 years. When built, she cost more than $332 million, a lot of money for a ship of the late 1950s. *Long Beach* needs many more men than modern cruisers and is not as efficient as later nuclear-powered ships. Because of these factors, she remains the only one of her class.

Launched in December 1974, the USS Virginia, *powered with two water-cooled nuclear reactors, is a more efficient design than the USS* Long Beach.

California And Virginia Classes

Cutting a choppy sea, the USS California clearly shows its design likeness to the Virginia class.

The six ships in these two classes are grouped together because they represent the best all-around cruisers in the modern U.S. Navy. For a while after the *Long Beach* was laid down, the navy shied away from funding more nuclear-powered ships, but the improvements made in reactor design and operating efficiency changed their minds. Named *California* and *South Carolina,* the two California-class vessels were ordered as nuclear-powered missile cruisers. Both were laid down in 1970; the *California* was launched in 1971, followed by her sister ship a year later.

With a multitude of radar and electronic devices to acquire and track air or surface threats, the ships are 596 feet long with a maximum displacement of 10,450 tons fully loaded. Each requires a crew of up to 44 officers and 559 enlisted men. Two geared turbines driven by the two pressurized water-cooled nuclear reactors provide a top speed of more than 30 knots.

Virginia-class boats carry a crew of approximately 40 officers and 570 enlisted men.

Considerable improvements have been made to radar carried by the Virginia-class cruisers, including special equipment to defeat jammers likely to be operated by enemy naval forces.

Weapon systems include eight Harpoon launchers in two batteries, 80 Standard SAM rounds fired from two launchers, two Phalanx point defense mounts, two 127mm (5-inch) saluting guns, six Mark 32 torpedo tubes, and one eight-tube ASW rocket launcher. The Standard missile rounds are carried in two magazines beneath the launchers. Plans exist to fit Tomahawk in a refit similar to that given the USS *Long Beach* .

Three more California-class cruisers were canceled because of the costs, but a decision to order more Nimitz-class aircraft carriers brought an order for modified California-class cruisers based on the Spruance-class destroyer. Four Virginia-class ships were built between 1972 and 1978, but a fifth was canceled. The Virginia-class ships are 11 feet shorter than the California class, their maximum displacement of 11,000 tons is slightly greater than *California*'s, and they have a slightly larger crew. The Virginia and California classes differ primarily in helicopter support, the Virginia class having hangar space below deck and a special elevator.

The armament of the Virginia class is the same as that fitted to the *California* and the *South Carolina,* but the *Virginia* and the *Arkansas* have already been adapted to carry eight Tomahawk SSMs, with *Mississippi* and *Texas* expected to receive Tomahawks in due course. Many improvements to the radar and electronics are taking place, upgrading these ships with the latest and most effective air and ship defense systems.

Virginia represents a good, all-around fleet defense and attack cruiser. She very nearly became the model for one of the most advanced anti-air systems yet devised, the Aegis. Four ships were ordered but later canceled in favor of a conventionally powered Ticonderoga class that was expected to get the Aegis system seaborne in less time and for less money.

The USS **Arkansas** *was launched in October 1978 and commissioned exactly two years later — the last of the Virginia-class nuclear-propelled guided-missile cruisers.*

Virginia-class boats have a hangar for helicopters installed beneath the fantail flight deck. A telescoping hatch cover and an electro-mechanical elevator transport helicopters between the main deck and the hangar.

MISSISSIPPI

Ticonderoga Class

If California- and Virginia-class ships represent good examples of typical cruiser capabilities, the USS *Ticonderoga* is a perfect example of specialization for a specific task. Beginning with major developments in missile technology during the 1960s, the U.S. Navy became increasingly concerned about the ability of its surface and sub-surface forces to survive attack. Attack from limited enemy forces at the disposal of little countries could be just as dangerous as those from major nations using the latest and most sophisticated weaponry.

A starboard bow view of the Aegis guided-missile cruiser USS Ticonderoga.

A lower angle bow view of the USS Ticonderoga *under way during sea trials.*

The USS Ticonderoga *was laid down in January 1980, launched in April 1981, and received its operational commission to serve in the Mediterranean Sea from January 1983.*

Because the United States relies increasingly on trade with many countries for its economic health and welfare, the warship today must be ready to defend both itself and the merchant fleets under its protection. With worldwide responsibilities, the naval force can be stretched thin, so each ship has to have many different capabilities. Each ship is very costly, extremely important, and has a specific set of duties to carry out.

Sometimes specific duties are so well defined that they call for a dedicated ship to carry them out with success. Such is the case with *Ticonderoga,* specially built to incorporate the Aegis combat system. Aegis is not a single piece of equipment, and on its own it can do nothing to protect the ships under its umbrella. Instead, it is a complete weapon control system using existing missiles to protect the surface fleet from attack more intelligently.

Powered by conventional gas-turbine engines, the USS Ticonderoga *carries a crew of 24 officers and approximately 334 enlisted men.*

The combat weapons controlled by Aegis include the surface-to-surface Standard missile to knock out enemy missiles, aircraft, and surface ships, the Phalanx automatic anti-air gun to destroy very fast anti-ship missiles or sea-skimming planes at close range, 127mm (5-inch) guns for close surface targets, Harpoon for attacking long-range surface threats, anti-submarine rockets (**ASROC**), torpedoes, airborne helicopters for ASW operations, and electronic decoys and detectors.

The clever thing about Aegis is that it connects and controls all these weapons from a series of advanced and highly sophisticated computers, which get their information from very advanced and highly capable radar antennas. Aegis ties the information together and decides which targets pose a genuine threat to the fleet under its protection, which are decoys sent out to look harmless, which are decoys trying to look offensive but in fact offer no threat, and which ships or

Under way during sea trials in the Gulf of Mexico, the USS **Mobile Bay** *leans to port while making a sharp right turn.*

aircraft have strayed into the potential battle area unaware of imminent action.

Clearly, a complex and sophisticated system like Aegis needed a very special type of ship, dedicated to the defense of several ships operating as a battle group of small merchant vessels threatened by enemy action. The *Ticonderoga,* based on the Spruance-class destroyer, emerged when earlier plans for Virginia-class ships were abandoned. The *Ticonderoga* was laid down in 1980, launched in April 1981, and joined the navy in 1983. It has a length of 566 feet, a beam of 55 feet, and a maximum loaded displacement of 9,600 tons. The ship has a complement of 24 officers and 334 enlisted men and a top speed of more than 30 knots.

As part of a long and extensive modernization program, Ticonderoga-class cruisers are equipped with LAMPS helicopters operated from hangar and deck space at the rear of the ship.

The Ticonderoga-class design is a modification of the Spruance-class and has the same basic hull and propulsion systems. ▼

Capable of more than 30 knots, Ticonderoga-class cruisers are equipped with eight Harpoon launchers and 88 Standard missiles. ▲

Conventionally powered, Aegis carries 88 Standard missiles, eight Harpoon launchers, two ASW rocket launchers, two Phalanx guns, two 127mm (5-inch) guns and two 40mm saluting guns. Large radars, sonar, and electronic intelligence-gathering equipment help the computers map everything within range of the ship's weapons. At present the navy has 13 Ticonderoga-class guided-missile cruisers, and from the sixth ship on, all vessels are fitted with Tomahawk launchers as well. Thus modified, each ship will carry 122 Harpoon, Standard, ASW, and Tomahawk missiles.

The USS Ticonderoga, *looking aft from the bow.*

The USS Yorktown *displays the clean lines typical of a Ticonderoga-class cruiser.*

The first three ships cost about $890 million each, but the cost was reduced to $835 million for the following three. The next three cost $931 million each, and each additional Ticonderoga-class vessel under construction in 1989 will not be completed for less than $920 million. The navy has invested more than 25 years of research and development and around $25,000 million in the 27 ships of this class it plans to have in service by the early 1990s. Yet even this enormous figure represents only 10 percent of the annual value in foreign trade, which these ships exist in part to help protect.

From the very beginning, the *Ticonderoga* came under heavy criticism. Some said that the enormous cost of each ship was too high a price for complex electronic and target detection systems that had yet to be shown workable. When the *Ticonderoga* put to sea for shakedown trials, critics pointed to her supposed poor performance. They called her a "gold-plated donkey," top heavy with too much equipment and so sophisticated she would never perform as advertised.

Yet when she began operational duty in the Mediterranean in 1984, *Ticonderoga* was seen to be a valuable asset. First, her very powerful radar surveillance systems monitored potential air threats over the carrier force. Then she was able to provide data for navy fighters intercepting the Egyptian airliner carrying the hijackers of the cruise ship *Achille Lauro* from Egypt to Tunisia.

In 1986, the Ticonderoga-class ships *Yorktown* and *Vincennes* centrally coordinated air action over the target when carrier planes and F-111s based in England successfully hit missile sites in Libya. Earlier that year they had controlled operations in the Gulf of Sidra, resulting in the sinking of two Libyan patrol boats. The Ticonderoga had demolished the negative views of its opponents. Even Congress changed its mind on earlier criticism and in 1987 added an Aegis cruiser to the President's budget request.

Sophisticated electronics and fire control systems can only be as good as the people that operate them. Information can be misunderstood or computers can misinterpret information from the radar systems and decoders. Such was the case when the USS *Vincennes* accidentally shot down an Iran Air Airbus airliner over the Persian Gulf on July 3, 1988. The *Vincennes* was under attack from gunboats, and its captain thought the Airbus was a plane attacking the cruiser.

Truxtun And Belknap Classes

Built during the early 1960s, the U.S. Navy also operates 9 Belknap-class guided-missile cruisers, each 547 feet long, with a beam of 55 feet and a maximum displacement of 8,250 tons. A nuclear-powered version, the USS *Truxtun,* launched in 1964, is slightly longer and has a maximum displacement of 9,127 tons. The Belknap class carries a complement of 479 while the Truxtun carries a crew of 561. In many other respects the ships are similar.

The Belknap cruiser carries one SH-2D LAMPS helicopter and a total crew of approximately 480 officers and men. ▶

Belknap-class cruisers were built between 1962 and 1965, a period in which nine ships of this class were laid down and launched.

Launched in July 1965, the USS Biddle was commissioned two years later.

Each Belknap-class ship carries eight Harpoon launchers in two locations, 60 Standard SAM rounds, a 127mm (5-inch) gun, two Phalanx defense systems, ASW rocket launchers, and two triple torpedo tubes. *Truxtun* has identical armament, with the exception of four fixed torpedo tubes. *Belknap* can carry one Kaman Aerospace SH-2 Seasprite helicopter equipped with search radar and **sonobuoys** for anti-submarine warfare.

Four Belknap ships are assigned duty in the Atlantic Ocean while five Belknap and the USS *Truxtun* are in the Pacific Ocean. Several modifications are planned for the years ahead, and all ten vessels are expected to remain on active service for a long time to come. They will probably not retire before the early part of the next century.

Smaller than Ticonderoga-class cruisers, the Belknap guided-missile cruisers are each powered by geared turbine engines, providing a maximum speed of 32.5 knots under ideal conditions.

Soviet Cruisers

Of the 40 Soviet cruisers operated by the Russian navy, no less than half are twenty years old or more. This is about the same percentage as the U.S. cruisers. The Soviet cruiser force, however, has more heavy ships with substantial missile armament. In addition, they have two 17,500-ton helicopter cruisers, although it is rumored that the Russians are not pleased with the design and are planning no more.

Excluding the two Moskva helicopter cruisers, the remaining 38 Soviet cruisers total a displacement of 441,400 tons, not significantly more than the 372, 316 tons of total U.S. cruiser displacement. Of the total Soviet tonnage, however, almost half (206,400 tons) is accounted for by the 12 Sverdlov ships, which have an emphasis on out-of-date guns and anti-aircraft missiles.

Dominating the deck line on this Soviet Slava-class guided-missile cruiser are launch tubes for sixteen SS-N-12 missiles.

All Soviet cruisers are powered by gas or steam turbines. They have no nuclear-powered cruisers. The latest Slava-class ships, however, carry 16 anti-ship missiles each with a range of 340 miles. *Slava* has a maximum displacement of 12,500 tons and a length of 613 feet. She carries 40 SAM rounds and facilities for one helicopter. *Slava* is believed to carry a crew of around 600 sailors and to have a creditable top speed of 34 knots.

The bulk of the Soviet cruiser fleet consists of Kara- and Kresta-class ships, displacing between 7,600 tons and 9,700 tons fully loaded. Kara ships carry 144 anti-ship, anti-submarine, and SAM rounds, with 10 torpedo tubes, 8 guns, and a battery of anti-submarine charges. They carry a crew of 540 and possess a range of 9,000 miles at a steady 15 knots. They can travel shorter distances faster, up to a maximum speed of 34 knots.

Far larger than any comparable U.S. cruiser, the Soviet Kirov battle cruiser has a displacement of approximately 28,000 tons fully loaded.

Cruiser Weapons

One of the most effective anti-ship missiles for cruiser use is the McDonnell Douglas Harpoon. Development began in the late 1960s on a missile that could attack surface targets with a high probability of destroying them. Designed initially to be launched by an aircraft, it was subsequently fitted to ships and even to submarines. To date, more than 5,000 Harpoons have been delivered to the U.S. Navy and many other countries. A number of Libyan boats in the Gulf of Sirte have been destroyed by Harpoon missiles.

Early versions of Harpoon had a range of about 80 miles, but improved models can hit targets 100 miles away. The missile is propelled by a small jet engine and achieves a maximum speed of about 640 MPH. It

Warships are not built to operate independently but as a functional part of a battle group formation, most probably involving an aircraft carrier, destroyers, cruisers, and frigates.

Protection of battle forces from attack by air is the special responsibility of Ticonderoga-class cruisers equipped with the Aegis fire-control system.

The large white cylinder behind this crew member is part of the Phalanx anti-aircraft weapon system.

is thrown into the air by a small solid-propellant rocket motor at the rear, which drops away and leaves the jet engine to continue the flight. Harpoon has a delayed action fuse so that the missile penetrates the target before exploding inside the ship. The warhead is a high explosive charge of almost 500 pounds.

Tests show that one Harpoon can destroy a small missile boat, two will stop a frigate, four will put a guided-missile cruiser out of action, and five will destroy a small carrier. Harpoon carries special electronic equipment to prevent it being jammed by enemy radar. U.S. cruisers carry Harpoon in vertical boxed launchers. The ship-launched version is 15 feet long with a diameter of 13.5 inches and a span across the small wings of 3 feet. With a small booster motor attached, it weighs 1,500 pounds.

Operating on generally similar principles to Harpoon, the General Dynamics BGM-109 Tomahawk is a cruise missile of tremendous potential. It is 21 feet long, 1 foot 9 inches in diameter and deploys wings that span 8 feet 4 inches. Hurled into the air by a small solid-propellant rocket motor, Tomahawk is propelled to its target by a small turbojet engine at a speed of around 525 MPH.

Missiles have largely replaced guns as the primary method of defense against other surface ships and attacking aircraft.

With a high explosive warhead, the BGM-109B anti-ship missile has a range of almost 300 miles. The missile can make several turns in flight to confuse enemy radar or observers about its destination. It has a 1,000-pound warhead and can achieve lethal results against all targets within range on land or at sea. It would be particularly effective against fast-moving guided-missile cruisers making sharp maneuvers to throw conventional missiles off target.

In the BGM-109A version Tomahawk carries a nuclear warhead which it can deliver to land targets 1,600 miles from the point of launch. With precise maps of the land over which it flies, the missile can make course corrections, continuously updating its navigation systems to achieve great accuracy. In these roles accuracy is measured in a few feet, and Tomahawk is able to put its warhead precisely on target. So far, the U.S. Navy has taken delivery of about 2,000 Tomahawk missiles.

To defend the cruiser against close-in attack from fast missiles, General Dynamics developed the Phalanx weapon system. It is built around a General Electric 20mm six-barrel Vulcan gatling gun, which is highly effective against almost anything that is likely to be thrown against a cruiser. Phalanx is being fitted to more than 360 ships in the U.S. Navy, from aircraft carriers to frigates.

The Phalanx is capable of detecting the incoming missile threatening the cruiser, tracking it, aligning the Vulcan gun on target and firing it, and maintaining track until it is destroyed. The gatling gun has breathtaking firepower and pumps the target with 3,000 rounds per minute. Every second it fires, 50 shells leave the barrels. There are very few missiles that could survive such a torrent of hot metal and still hit the ship.

Phalanx has an effective range of almost a mile, but it can continue to track and fire when the target is

The combination of the Aegis fire-control system and rapid-launched missiles housed in vertical canisters makes the Ticonderoga guided-missile cruiser a formidable defense system.

A Ticonderoga-class guided-missile cruiser, the USS Antietam, test-fires a live anti-aircraft missile from its vertical launch system. ▶

close in, hitting it from a range of only 1,500 feet. When the six-barrel gun is aligned with the target, a short burst is usually sufficient. If the target is not destroyed, the electronics tracking the target detect this and fire the gun again.

The Standard surface-to-air missile protects the carrier against air threats. It is 27 feet long and powered by a powerful rocket motor. The missile weighs about 3,000 pounds and has a range of approximately 90 miles with a maximum speed of Mach 2.5 (2.5 times the speed of sound). Standard can hit planes at an altitude of up to 65,000 feet, and it forms the core of the air defense equipment not only on cruisers but also on other types of U.S. warships.

The Soviet Slava cruisers carry 16 SS-N-12 Sandbox anti-ship missiles, each approximately 38 feet long. Powered by a turbojet engine, they are controlled by a radio command and a radar homing device that puts the warhead accurately on target. The missile can carry a nuclear warhead or a 2.2-ton conventional charge across a range of about 340 miles.

Slava-class cruisers first appeared with the Sandbox missile in 1982. Before that it was seen only on the small Kiev aircraft carriers, and some submarines have been reported to carry it. The Soviets have always liked cruise missiles and were the first to develop weapons of this type in large numbers during the 1940s and 1950s. The Sandbox is not particularly sophisticated but represents a comparatively formidable threat to large ships.

With ever more effective weapons and sophisticated electronic systems to control them, the cruiser has a long future ahead of it. In wartime it would be a remarkably effective fighting ship, protecting the large naval battle groups and operating as an advanced attack vessel on its own. In peace, it is equally important as a visible demonstration of America's willingness to protect its merchant fleets and those of its allies.

◀ Bunker Hill, *the sixth ship in the Ticonderoga class, became the first U.S. warship to test-fire missiles from the vertical launch system in May 1986.*

Three anti-aircraft missiles race away from the forward deck magazines of the USS Bunker Hill *during a rapid-fire test launch.* ▶

Abbreviations

ASROC	Anti-Submarine Rocket
ASW	Anti-Submarine Warfare
SAM	Surface-To-Air Missile
SSM	Surface-To-Surface Missile
USS	United States Ship
	Designation for a warship of the United States Navy, such as USS *Bronstein*.

Glossary

Bauxite

A clay-like substance that is the main mineral in aluminum.

Displacement

The measure of the size of a ship, given by the amount of water it displaces. Figures given in this book are for "full-load displacement," when the ship is fully armed, equipped, and loaded for war.

Knot

The measure of speed at sea.
1 knot = 1 nautical mile per hour.

Nautical mile

1 nautical mile = 1.1515 statute miles
= 6.082 feet

Sonobuoys

Small cylindrical devices used to detect submerged submarines by the noise they emit.

Index

Page references in *italics* indicate photographs or illustrations.